Daniel Boone

and the Exploration
of the Frontier

Explorers of New Worlds

Daniel Boone

and the Exploration
of the Frontier

Richard Kozar

Chelsea House Publishers
Philadelphia

Prepared for Chelsea House Publishers by:
OTTN Publishing, Warminster PA

CHELSEA HOUSE PUBLISHERS
Editor in Chief: Stephen Reginald
Managing Editor: James D. Gallagher
Production Manager: Pamela Loos
Art Director: Sara Davis
Director of Photography: Judy L. Hasday
Senior Production Editor: LeeAnne Gelletly
Series Designer: Keith Trego

3 5 7 9 8 6 4 2

Library of Congress Cataloging-in-Publication Data

Kozar, Richard.
    Daniel Boone and the exploration of the frontier / by
    Richard F. Kozar.
p.   cm. – (Explorers of new worlds)
Includes bibliographical references and index.
Summary: Presents a biography of the legendary fron-
tiersman who explored Kentucky and the route to the
West leading to American expansion of the United States.
ISBN 0-7910-5510-8 (hc)
1. Boone, Daniel, 1734–1820 Juvenile literature. 2. Pio-
neers–Kentucky Biography Juvenile literature. 3. Fron-
tier and pioneer life–Kentucky Juvenile literature. 4.
Kentucky Biography Juvenile literature. 5. Kentucky–
Discovery and exploration Juvenile literature. 6. Mis-
souri–Discovery and exploration Juvenile literature. [1.
Boone, Daniel, 1734–1820. 2. Pioneers.] I. Title. II.
Series.
F454.B66K68   1999
976.9'02'092–dc21   99-22259
[B]   CIP
                                                AC

Contents

Exploring the
Wild Frontier

This well-known painting by George Caleb Bingham shows Daniel Boone leading a party of settlers through the Cumberland Gap. Boone discovered this pathway to the west through the Appalachian Mountains, and helped guide America's expansion in the 18th and 19th centuries.

I

oday, the word ***frontier*** may seem like a strange term. It means the farthest point of civilization or settlement. The reason people seldom think of frontiers anymore is that, except for the deepest parts of the ocean and the unexplored regions of outer space, the world no longer has any frontiers. But a little over two centuries ago in America, much of the country was considered frontier, believe it or not.

During the 18th century, the land west of the Ohio River was rarely traveled by people other than Native Americans—which is the main reason white settlers avoided the wilderness in the first place. For although not every tribe was hostile, many of the Indians did consider "palefaces" to be intruders who threatened their food supply and traditional way of life. To these tribes, the only good white man was a dead one.

However, despite the dangers of the mid-1700s, there were adventuresome men who weren't afraid to seek out and explore parts of this country where no white man had gone before. They were called *frontiersmen*, and one of the most famous was Daniel Boone.

Boone was happiest exploring and living in the wilderness, far away from the hustle and bustle of civilization. And civilization to him wasn't colonial Philadelphia or Boston, where men and women wore the latest European fashions and lived in brick or stone houses. No, he was famous for moving farther west as soon as he could smell the smoke rising from a new neighbor's log cabin.

Not that Daniel didn't try to live like other men of his day. For a while, he did his best to scratch out a living as a farmer. But before long, it was plain that he wasn't really happy living off the land in such fashion. The only way he wanted to live off the land was by hunting squirrel, wild turkey, and deer, and trapping fox, raccoon, and beaver for their valuable furs, which were in demand in colonial America and Europe. And what set his heart pumping was the thought of seeing what was over the next mountain or down the unexplored rivers of America. To men like Boone, the grass was always greener on the other side of the mountain. And as long as there were new mountains to cross, he was happy to **trek** over them.

What legacy did he leave behind? That of a restless explorer who was seldom content to stay in one place for long, but one whose **wanderlust** led early American settlers to follow him. Men like Daniel Boone were trailblazers, fearless individuals who risked life and limb to tame the frontier. Most of all, they weren't afraid to leave a relatively peaceful, safe, and civilized life behind. Ironically, however, the very wilderness they explored and conquered was soon populated with land-hungry settlers, the very kind of civilized folk that led Boone to keep heading westward in search of new horizons.

Grass Is Always Greener

Explorers of New Worlds

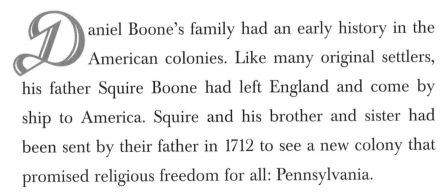

William Penn meets with a group of Native Americans in Philadelphia, the town he established in his North American colony. Penn was a member of a religious group known as Quakers; Daniel Boone, who was born in Pennsylvania, also was a Quaker.

2

aniel Boone's family had an early history in the American colonies. Like many original settlers, his father Squire Boone had left England and come by ship to America. Squire and his brother and sister had been sent by their father in 1712 to see a new colony that promised religious freedom for all: Pennsylvania.

The Boones were members of a religious group called **Quakers**. This group refused to belong to the Church of

This house in Berks County, Pennsylvania, stands on the site of the cabin where Daniel Boone was born in 1734.

England, their country's official religion. They also refused to fight in wars, and felt they did not need priests or ministers to communicate with God. In England during the 17th and early 18th centuries, Quakers were **persecuted** for their religious beliefs.

A fellow Quaker named William Penn had founded Pennsylvania in 1682. The Boone family was naturally drawn to the colony's vast forests and fertile valleys. Squire Boone and his siblings sent a message about the colony to their father, and the rest of the Boone family arrived in 1717.

From the moment they set foot in the New World, the Boones were determined to own their own property. This was something that only the very wealthiest people could do in England. The Boones eventually ended up in Berks County. Their farm was on the edge of the explored area of the colony, even though it was not far from Philadelphia, the center of commerce and government in Pennsylvania and an important colonial city.

In 1720, Squire Boone married a Quaker named Sarah Morgan. Squire was a ***weaver*** by trade (someone who makes blankets and fabric by "weaving" wool, cotton, or linen on a loom). But by the time Daniel, the sixth of Sarah and Squire's 11 children, was born on November 2, 1734, his enterprising father had also set up a blacksmith's shop on his 25-acre homestead and grazed cattle.

However, Daniel was always more interested in the woods and in hunting the wild animals that lived there than he was in farming. He spent every possible minute exploring the outdoors.

Unlike most of his brothers and sisters, Daniel's formal schooling was limited; however, his knowledge of life in the woods was vast. By the time he was a teenager, he had become such an excellent shot with a rifle that he was repairing guns in his father's blacksmith shop and supplying wild *game* for the Boone dinner table.

Daniel exhibited a daring as a young man that would be a characteristic throughout his life, and unlike the normally peaceful Quakers, he refused to back down from a fight. Actually, by 1750 the entire Boone clan had found Quaker life so restrictive that they decided to leave their farm in Pennsylvania and move south through Virginia to North Carolina, where they had heard that

> **Although Quakers were pacifists who opposed war, in America not all Quakers chose to avoid guns. The lives of people living on the frontier often depended on their ability to handle a weapon.**

rich land abounded. The family set up a new homestead near the Yadkin River, on the very outskirts of colonial America.

Because the Boones were living at the edge of the wilderness, they were periodically threatened by Indian tribes. The Native Americans did not appreciate white men invading their hunting grounds, and did not respect the settlers' claims to the land. Although some tribes were peaceful, the Cherokee

This letter is the longest piece of Daniel Boone's writing
that exists. Although Boone had little "book learning,"
he knew a great deal about surviving in the wilderness.

and Shawnee could attack colonists without warning when they felt threatened.

The Indians also fought among themselves over
hunting rights and other issues. Worse, during this

time England and France were challenging each other over unsettled areas of North America.

The British controlled 13 colonies stretching along the coast of the Atlantic Ocean, from Maine to Georgia. France, on the other hand, laid claim to eastern Canada, the Great Lakes, much of the Midwest, and south along the Mississippi River to the Gulf of Mexico. And what they fiercely disputed were the fertile plains and valleys of the Ohio River, where animals like beavers and otter—valuable for their fur—lived in great abundance.

To strengthen its claim there, France began establishing outposts in the disputed Ohio River territory. The French hoped this would keep the British colonists from moving farther west. However, since England had already built trading posts along the upper Ohio River Valley, conflict was bound to break out eventually.

The French were formidable opponents for the British. Because the French had gone out of their way to

France controlled a larger part of North America than England did. However, the English colonists heavily outpopulated the French —two million English versus approximately 80,000 French in 1756.

befriend most Indians and trade with them (French trappers even married Indian squaws and lived among their tribes), they convinced many Indians to be their *allies*. Only the Iroquois, a powerful Indian nation in New York, Pennsylvania, and the Ohio Valley, sided with the British.

In the winter of 1753, a 21-year-old Virginia *militia* (civilian army) officer named George Washington was ordered by his British superiors to cross 500 miles of wilderness and tell the French commander at Fort LeBoeuf on Lake Erie to leave the region. When the French officer refused, Washington was given command of 159 men and sent back early the next year to establish British rights along the Ohio.

After a successful *skirmish* with a French scouting party, the soldiers built a *stockade*, Fort Necessity, at the site where the Allegheny and Monongahela Rivers merge to form the Ohio. (Today, this is the location of the city of Pittsburgh.) Unfortunately, because the hastily constructed fort had been built in a valley, the French and Indians simply hid in the woods overlooking the stockade and fired at will on the English. Washington lost a third of his men and was forced to retreat to Virginia.

In the wilderness, Daniel Boone's best friend was his rifle, which he nicknamed "Old Lick-Ticker."

The Adventures Begin

3

ecause the Ohio River's forks were a **strategic** location, the French promptly built their own stockade there, naming it Fort Duquesne. In 1755, the British forces returned to reclaim the site. This time, the troops were led by English general Edward Braddock. Among the trained soldiers and militiamen was a 20-year-old wagon driver named Daniel Boone.

George Washington and the colonial militiamen had grave doubts about Braddock's battle plan. The general intended to attack as if he were marching on the wide open plains of Europe against traditional military foes. But the

The overconfident British General Braddock refused to listen to George Washington and Benjamin Franklin.

French and Indians weren't about to go head-to-head against the British in plain view. Instead, they intended to use the woods and rocks as cover while they picked off their enemies one by one.

Even the wise colonist Benjamin Franklin, who helped outfit Braddock's force with guns and cannon, had cautioned him about waging a European battle in America's forests. In his autobiography, Franklin said Braddock "smil'd at my Ignorance, and reply'd 'These Savages may indeed be a formidable enemy to your raw American Militia; but upon the King's regular and disciplin'd troops, Sir, it is impossible they should make any impression.'"

In order to wage his campaign against the French, Braddock had his force blaze a wide trail through western Pennsylvania so his rows of men and cannon could make the trek more easily. However, doing this warned the French about the advancing British army.

On July 9, 1755, Braddock's men were marching on a trail when Indians opened fire from hiding places. Many of the British soldiers were cut down before the party ever got within sight of Fort Duquesne. As the redcoats began dropping, the surviving soldiers panicked. Many broke ranks and ran away. As Braddock furiously tried to reassemble his troops, he was mortally wounded in the chest by a bullet. Washington himself had two horses shot out from under him, and was nearly hit in the head with a bullet. The French and Indian War, as it became known, had officially begun.

The regular soldiers of the British army wore bright-red military uniforms (hence the nickname "redcoats"). The soldiers were as colorful as cardinals—and made brilliant targets for French and Indian sharpshooters.

Many of the survivors of the *massacre* retreated back over the mountains to Albany, New York. As for Daniel Boone, he was at the rear of the action when the fighting began, and when he and his fellow woodsmen saw Indians racing after retreating redcoats, they grabbed the nearest horses and took off themselves for the safety of the woods. Daniel eventually made it back to North Carolina and his family farm.

Another adventure had already begun forming in young Boone's mind. Always anxious to explore new country and stake a claim on new land, he began to dream of heading over the mountains to a new region known as Kentucky, where game and fur-bearing animals supposedly flourished and fertile land was just waiting for bold men to stake claim to it. Because people on the frontier always dreamed of greener pastures beyond where they lived, they began to think of Kentucky as "paradise."

But Boone also had other things on his mind. He was interested in a young lady named Rebecca Bryan. Rebecca was the sister of his brother-in-law, William Bryan. Following Daniel's escape from Braddock's disastrous campaign against the French, he began courting Rebecca, a pretty girl who was four years younger than his own 21 years. Daniel sought to impress his prospective bride and in-laws with his handiwork as a hunter by bringing a freshly killed deer to Rebecca's home and butchering it while she observed.

The early-morning sun colors the fog over Kentucky's Appalachian Mountains. Boone and other adventurers saw Kentucky as a paradise waiting to be explored.

While this may not be something a couple would do on a date today, in Daniel Boone's time a man was expected to provide for his family, either by farming or hunting. And skill with a gun was more valuable than being handy with a horse plow, at least on the frontier. A seasoned woodsman like Boone stood to earn far more than a farmer, who spent much of his time clearing trees, stumps, and rocks from soil, and the rest of the time tried to make meager crops grow in the cleared ground.

A hunter, who might kill four or five deer a day, could receive a dollar apiece (or a "buck") for the hides. Boone reportedly could kill 30 deer a day. Beaver and otter pelts were worth even more, between $3 and $5 dollars a pelt. A long winter of successful trapping, therefore, could easily earn a frontiersman more income than he could make in a whole year of farming. So the blood-spattered Boone was more of a catch for a frontier lady than he might seem at first glance.

Luckily, Rebecca didn't faint at the sight of blood, and she was perfectly capable of doing all the household chores a frontier wife was expected to do. These included raising her children, making and washing their clothes, cooking wild game for dinner, planting and harvesting vegetables, educating her youngsters, and even using a musket if Indians threatened her family.

Daniel and Rebecca were married on August 14, 1756. Together, they would raise 10 children. (Although this would be a remarkably large family today, in colonial days it was not unusual for families to have that many children.) Initially, the newlyweds lived in a log cabin on Daniel's father's property, but eventually they moved several miles away to a site near Sugar Tree Creek, where they remained, except during Indian uprisings, for the next 10 years.

For a time, Daniel took up farming on his land, although not very enthusiastically, and he also drove wagons pulled by teams of horses. But true to his woodsman's nature, he preferred to spend the fall and winter months on lengthy hunting trips.

In 1758, however, he once again joined a British *campaign* against the French at Fort Duquesne. This time, the British were led by General John Forbes. Like Braddock, the general cut a trail through the wilderness—known as the Forbes Road—to engage England's enemies in the Ohio River Valley. Fortunately, this time around the British fared better than they had under Braddock. Of course, it helped that Forbes's forces outnumbered the French by five to one. When the French commander realized his weak position, he ordered his forces to retreat and destroyed Fort Duquesne. Forbes laid claim to the site, and named the area Pittsburgh, after William Pitt, the English nobleman who was in charge of the British war effort.

A monument to Daniel Boone shows the woodsman fighting with an Indian. During Boone's life he was involved in many fights with the Native Americans; he killed his first Indian while marching with General Forbes to attack Fort Duquesne.

Many years later, Daniel would say that his most vivid memory of the campaign was when he killed his first Indian near the Juniata River in central Pennsylvania. According the the woodsman, the Indian leaped out of the underbrush and attacked him. Boone grabbed the brave and heaved him over a cliff.

While Daniel thrived on such excitement, his parents were growing weary of the threat of Indian attacks in North Carolina, so they left their homestead and moved back north to Maryland. Their new colony was more civilized than North Carolina at that time. Even Daniel agreed to seek a safer home, and in 1759 he packed up Rebecca and his two young sons in a wagon and moved to Culpeper County in the Shenandoah Valley of Virginia. But before he departed, he purchased 640 acres of Yadkin River land from his father, and returned there periodically to hunt, trap, and defend settlers against Cherokee Indian attacks.

The Call of Kentucky

Daniel Boone and five companions—John Finley, John Stuart, Joseph Holden, William Cooley, and Ames Mooney—gaze at the "paradise" to the west: Kentucky.

4

When the frontiersmen finally defeated the Cherokee in North Carolina in 1760, temporary peace returned. Daniel brought Rebecca and their children back to the Yadkin River land. He began farming again, but apparently not with much zest. As always, he took far greater pleasure in hunting and other adventures, such as chasing thieves who had been harassing the local settlers and saving a young girl who had been kidnapped.

Indeed, the prospect of adventure is what easily convinced Daniel in the spring of 1765 to join an expedition made up of several old militia buddies. They intended to head overland to Florida, a former Spanish territory that had just been bought by the British. England offered land there free to any Protestant settlers in the colonies. This was an opportunity men like Boone couldn't pass up. When he bid farewell to Rebecca, he estimated he would be home in time for Christmas dinner.

Nearly every man on the 500-mile trip through the Southern wilderness found Florida a nightmare instead of a paradise. In those days, it was little more than a swamp-filled region populated mostly by snakes, insects, and Indians. Only Boone found the Pensacola area they reached attractive, and he decided to acquire land there.

True to his promise, on Christmas day, as his family was sitting down to dinner, an enthusiastic Daniel burst into the cabin. He told them all about Florida's countryside—then announced that the family would soon be headed there permanently. This time, however, Rebecca refused to uproot her family and move to a place she knew so little about. Boone had no choice but to drop his plans.

So once again, the lure of Kentucky began to call Daniel Boone. Unfortunately, the end of the French and Indian War in 1763 led Britain to stop encouraging colonists to settle and populate frontier lands. The conflict that had started as a skirmish at Fort Duquesne had expanded to a full-fledged war that ended up being waged on the high seas and around the globe. The war was very expensive to the British. Also, England's rush to populate frontier America had infuriated the Indian tribes who were pushed out in the process, leading them to fight the British tooth and nail.

Therefore, England had issued the Proclamation of 1763, which attempted to prevent colonists from moving into regions west of the Appalachian Mountains and into the Ohio River territory. But the colonists in early America were growing more independent when it came to matters such as land ownership restrictions and taxation—especially when there was land to be claimed and money to be made from the fur trade. The fabled region of Kentucky was looking better and better all the time.

Daniel traveled to Kentucky twice in 1767. The first occasion was a hunting and trapping trip. But even an experienced woodsman like Daniel Boone

When Daniel Boone and his brother, Squire, arrived in Kentucky, they were amazed at the beautiful landscape.

wasn't completely safe from hostile Indians. He and his partner were robbed of their furs by several Cherokee. Later that fall, Daniel and his brother Squire returned for a longer stay, spending the winter on the west side of the Blue Ridge Mountains. The pair were amazed at the beautiful landscape of Kentucky, as well as the endless stands of oak, maple, pine, walnut, and hickory timber.

The following winter, John Finley, a frontiersman who had been one of the first Americans to explore Kentucky from Pennsylvania via the Ohio River 14 years earlier, sought out Boone in North Carolina. He had married one of Daniel's sisters, and now had a proposal for her woodsman brother. Finley was convinced there had to be a "gap" through the Cumberland Mountains through which men like themselves could reach Kentucky traveling overland from North Carolina and Virginia, just as easily as Pennsylvanians could get there down the Ohio River. Because Finley felt Daniel was a more experienced trailblazer, he asked him to lead the expedition.

Boone, naturally, couldn't resist the offer, even though part of the trip through Kentucky would be along an old trail that was used by the Cherokee when they traveled north to make war with other tribes. With four other men—John Stuart, Joseph Holden, William Cooley, and Ames Mooney—Boone and Finley set off in May 1769.

Natural explorer that he was, Boone found the fabled Cumberland Gap and led the men through it into present-day Kentucky, near the southwestern tip of Virginia. Once they entered "paradise," the hunters and trappers eagerly set out to accumulate as many furs and skins as they could, hoping to make a hefty profit when they returned to civilization.

At one point, Daniel and John Stuart separated from the other men to cover more countryside in their travels. But while hunting along the Kentucky River late in December, they bumped into a war party of Shawnee and Delaware warriors on horseback, led by a fierce native named Chief Will.

In the French and Indian War, Chief Will had sided with the French against the British. He and his warriors made the two hunters take them back to the main camp. When they got there, the Indians promptly helped themselves to the men's furs, guns, ammunition, and horses. Luckily, the Indians left Boone and his friends with their scalps intact, along with a warning not to trespass in the region again.

But Daniel wasn't easily scared off. He and Stuart trailed the departing Indians. They even managed to recover some of their party's horses. However, Boone and his companion were once again captured by the warriors, who, miraculously, again spared his life—but took him all the way to the Ohio River before abandoning him and Stuart in the wilderness.

Not surprisingly, Boone and Stuart nonetheless

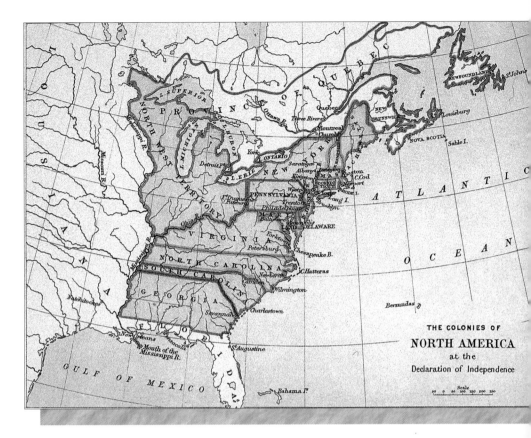

In 1763, England issued laws to prevent American colonists from moving west of the Appalachian Mountains. However, by the American Revolution 13 years later, each of the colonies had expanded westward.

found their way back to the other four frontiersmen, who had already given them up for dead. And to Daniel's surprise, he discovered that his brother Squire had joined the men, bringing fresh horses and the supplies that they needed. Freshly **outfitted**, Boone and Stuart decided to spend the winter in

> **From all accounts, John Stuart didn't make it through the winter of 1769–70. Although no one is certain, he probably was killed by Indians.**

Kentucky and take their chances with the Indians. The two men weren't anxious to be captured again, so they avoided the path used so frequently by the Cherokee. Instead, they set off in different directions along the Kentucky River, with Squire joining Daniel at least part of the time. In the spring of 1770, Squire packed up the *pelts* he and Daniel had collected. He returned to North Carolina to sell them and buy more supplies.

Although John Stuart was gone–probably dead–by this time, Daniel stayed in Kentucky to learn as much about the wilderness as possible. He was more careful than ever not to be captured by Indians again. However, in one famous tale, he found himself trapped by warriors at the edge of a cliff. Rather than surrender and hope for the best, he leaped off the edge of the bluff and fell some 60 feet into the lofty limbs of a treetop. Fortunately, the branches broke his fall. From the tree, he was able to climb to the ground and escape.

Another time, however, he wasn't as fortunate,

and again found himself caught–and released–by Chief Will. Perhaps the chief was in a good mood, for a few days earlier he had captured over a dozen frontiersmen and relieved them of every possession of value–well over 1,000 furs, their rifles, horses, traps, and even their dogs.

If Daniel felt grateful for his life, he didn't return the favor on his next trip to North Carolina. When he and Squire ran into a pair of Indians who were wearing silver jewelry, they killed them both and helped themselves to the silver and their weapons. After nearly two years away from his family in the wilderness, it was all he had to show for his absence.

A Land
of Plenty

The Cumberland Gap at sunrise. American colonists soon followed Boone's trail west through the Appalachian Mountains to Kentucky. The growing number of settlers soon found themselves battling Native Americans, who did not want to give up their land to the whites.

5

fter having been gone so long, Daniel likely felt obliged to spend some time with Rebecca and his growing family during the early 1770s. But he was constantly tempted by the land over the westward mountains, especially since other pioneers were rushing into the Ohio Valley and Kentucky by way of Pittsburgh and the Ohio River. One of them was George Rogers Clark, another young man with a thirst for adventure. After traveling 300

The dashing frontiersman George Rogers Clark (standing in the doorway at right) would become one of the heroes of the American Revolution. On July 4, 1778, he and his men captured a British outpost in the Ohio Valley territory without firing a shot. His younger brother, William Clark (left) would eventually gain fame as a leader of the Lewis and Clark expedition.

miles by canoe down the Ohio, he had staked a claim on terrain a friend described as "a Bottom of fine land on the Ohio which would be Valuable were it not for being so Surrounded with mountains surpassing anything you ever saw."

Interestingly, Clark's younger brother, William, had the heart of an explorer as well: several decades later he and a man named Meriwether Lewis would travel thousands of miles up the Missouri River, across the Rocky Mountains, and west to the Pacific Ocean in search of the fabled Northwest Passage.

Some settlers were also reaching the Ohio River Valley overland, along the roads built by generals Braddock and Forbes. A good deal of these folks were Virginians, who had been urged by their governor, Lord Dunmore, to lay claim to as much land as possible and thus expand Virginia's holdings. In those days, people from the 13 original colonies competed as much with each other as with the French to grab land on the frontier.

In early 1773, Boone once again returned to Kentucky. He decided it was time to move his entire family over the mountains. That fall, he packed up Rebecca and the children and set out along a narrow Indian trail–not wide enough for a wagon– to reach Kentucky. But before long, tragedy interrupted his quest. Daniel's oldest son, James, and his son's 16-year-old friend, Robert McAfee, were scouting ahead of the main group when they were attacked by Shawnee Indians. The youths were wounded by the warriors and then horribly tortured and killed. The families buried the slain teens, and then turned back for North Carolina.

The slayings enraged pioneers throughout the frontier, and they answered back with **atrocities** of their own against the Shawnee nation, including the slaughter of innocent Indian women and children.

As was customary, several other Indian tribes, such as the Cherokee, joined forces with the Shawnee against the white settlers. Their leader was a chief known as Cornstalk. To defend themselves, Daniel and others joined the Virginia Militia. The militia eventually defeated Cornstalk's warriors in a decisive battle in present-day West Virginia.

In the spring of 1775, Daniel once again led a group of land-hungry settlers to a site on the south bank of the Kentucky River. To do so, he had to

Daniel Boone's "Wilderness Road" from Virginia to the Ohio River became the main route for settlers moving westward into Kentucky.

blaze a trail of his own, which came to be known as the "Wilderness Road." Running from Virginia to the Ohio River, the road became the principal route for settlers streaming westward in Conestoga wagons over the next several decades. Appropriately, Daniel named the new Kentucky settlement Boonesborough.

Seven settlers were picked off by Indian riflemen as the pioneers made the treacherous overland trip along the Wilderness Road, but Boone and the others persevered. They even built a log fort for protection, and erected their cabins between the fort and the nearby Kentucky River.

Despite the settlement of Boonesborough, life on the frontier continued to be anything but settled. Competing colonies like North Carolina, Virginia, and Pennsylvania argued over who really had rightful claim to the lands of Kentucky, and settlers from all three staked claims in the region. Moreover, the Indians were constantly making deals with the frontiersmen over land. Sometimes, even the Indians did not have a right to the land in the first place!

Worst of all, by 1775, the first shots of the Revolutionary War between the colonies and Great Britain had been fired, which would lead a year later to the writing of the Declaration of Independence. England, which had long treated the eastern Indian nations with contempt, now encouraged them to be allies and attack the *rebellious* colonists.

At first, the men who had cleared the forests in Kentucky did not feel the revolutionary mood sparked in places like Boston and Philadelphia.

They wanted to remain loyal to England. Nonetheless, the pioneers banded together in the wilderness and even petitioned the new Continental Congress to recognize their claims in Kentucky.

But with hostile Indians attacking them from the north and south, most settlers decided Kentucky wasn't worth losing their scalps over. They retreated back over the mountains to the relative safety of the homes they had left. By the late summer of 1775, only 50 settlers remained in Kentucky. All were men.

Daniel remained committed to Boonesborough. In the fall of 1775, he went back to North Carolina to get Rebecca and his seven children, then returned to the Kentucky frontier. As word spread that families were back in Kentucky,

In 1775, Rebecca Boone and her daughter Jemima became the first white women to stand on the banks of the Kentucky River. This historic event proclaimed that Boonesborough was to become a permanent settlement, rather than a remote outpost filled with restless hunters and trappers.

especially during such hazardous times, other settlers followed suit and also headed west over the mountains.

Triumphs and Heartaches

Life on the frontier was filled with constant danger. Daniel Boone's daughter Jemima and two of her friends were kidnapped by Shawnee braves while boating on the Kentucky River. Fortunately, Daniel and other frontiersmen were able to rescue the young women. Over the next few years, though, two of Boone's brothers and three of his children were killed by Indians

6

rontier life involved constant hardship. Merely finding or growing enough food to eat was a daily chore. Luckily, Kentucky was filled with buffalo, deer, and wild turkey, and the fertile soil there made farming easy. But a peaceful day of frontier life could turn bloody in a moment when Indians decided to launch a surprise attack.

In July 1776, the same month that Congress issued the Declaration of Independence in Philadelphia, 14-year-old

Jemima Boone, Daniel's daughter, was canoeing with two of her female friends when they beached on the far shore of the Kentucky River, in Indian country. There, Shawnee warriors who had been eying the young girls rushed into the water. They captured the trio and began carrying them away.

However, the girls were clever enough to leave clues along the trail, which their anxious fathers and other woodsmen quickly discovered. Before long, the posse caught up with the struggling Indians, shot two of the warriors, and returned the girls safely to the settlement.

Meanwhile, Kentucky remained a battleground. On Dec. 25, 1776, Daniel and a large party of hunters were nearly overrun by more than 50 Mingo warriors. The hunters barely made it back to the still-incomplete fort at Boonesborough. Fearing for their lives, over half the pioneer families in Kentucky fled east over the Cumberland Mountains. Of those who

The kidnapping and rescue of Daniel Boone's daughters eventually inspired author James Fenimore Cooper, a famous early American novelist, to include a story about abducted maidens in his 1826 epic *The Last of the Mohicans.*

chose to stay, only 12 were females, including Rebecca and Jemima Boone.

Shawnee chief Blackfish was particularly determined, launching attack after attack against the American settlements. On April 24, 1777, the Shawnee tried all day to overrun the Boonesborough fort. Daniel himself would have been killed on several occasions if not for the help of his good friend Simon Kenton, a frontiersman and scout.

Typically, the Indians made surprise attacks to terrorize the settlers, rather than all-out offensives like at Boonesborough. Such tactics were meant to keep the pioneers on edge at all times. Boone described them as "mischiefs." Often, the Indians made frontier life nearly unbearable simply by killing the settlers' livestock or burning their crops.

Even Daniel grew weary of the harassment at one point. He noted in his autobiography, "I thought it was hard times, no bread, no salt, no vegetables, no fruit of any kinds, no ardent spirits, nothing but meat." Without salt as a *preservative*, especially in the spring and summer, even wild game was of little use after a short time because the meat would spoil. A bushel of salt in Kentucky was more valuable than a cow in those days.

It was on a salt-gathering mission in February (salt could be collected by boiling down salty water from certain springs or creeks) that Daniel embarked on one of his most dangerous—and *controversial*—adventures. While out hunting and checking traps, he was captured by several Indian braves. Daniel learned that a much larger war party intended to attack a group of his fellow frontiersmen. Chief Will, who had often spared Boone's life in the past, was among those in the party.

By fast talking, Daniel convinced his captors not to attack the rest of his men, saying they would become "adopted" members of the Shawnee. (Indians sometimes took whites into their tribes to replace warriors who died in battle. In addition, the British paid up to $100 for every American colonist turned over by the Indians.)

The following day, the 26 men in Boone's expedition were surrounded, but Daniel convinced them to surrender without a shot fired. Over half were eventually adopted by the Shawnee, and the others were turned over to the British in Detroit.

During the four months he spent with his Shawnee "brothers," Daniel learned they planned to attack the settlement in Boonesborough. The fol-

Daniel Boone was accused of making a deal with the Shawnee Indians after his capture and escape in 1777.

lowing June, he took a chance on a hunting trip, stole a horse, and raced across the wilderness—160 miles in four days—to warn the settlers in Kentucky.

Several settlers wondered how he had managed to escape while their husbands, fathers, and brothers were still in **captivity**. Many people suspected Daniel had made a deal. Worse, Boone learned that Rebecca, fearing he was long dead, had packed up their children (except daughter Jemima) and returned to her father's land in North Carolina.

Fearing a massive attack, Daniel urged the remaining settlers to finish the fort and prepare for a battle. In early September, over 400 Indians appeared at Boonesborough to wage the attack. For nearly two weeks, the warriors laid siege to the fort, even attempting to burn it to the ground. But on the 11th day, they gave up and retreated.

But Daniel's troubles weren't over. Because of suspicions over his dealings with the Shawnee, he was **court-martialed** (tried by a military court). At least some people were convinced he had helped plan the attack on Boonesborough. Nonetheless, the court ultimately found him innocent. In fact, his rank in the militia was raised from captain to major.

In late 1778, Daniel traveled once again back to North Carolina to a relieved Rebecca and his children. In October of the following year, they all returned to Kentucky—along with an estimated 20,000 other settlers who traveled down the Ohio and over the Wilderness Road. There, Daniel tried to establish rightful claims to 1,400 acres for himself and another 2,400 for his brother George and son Israel. Subsequently, he sold this land and planned to return to Virginia to arrange claims on even more frontier land (staking, buying, and selling land on the frontier to build one's wealth was common).

All told, Daniel was carrying an estimated $40,000 to $50,000 in his saddlebags (some of the money raised from friends' land sales) on the trip when he was apparently robbed along the way. As a result, he was financially ruined, as well as devastated over the loss of his friends' money.

As always, however, Daniel survived another frontier hardship. The truth is, he would face far worse. Before the Indian Wars died down in 1794, he would lose two brothers, Edward and Squire, and three children to marauding Indians. Finally, though, life on the Kentucky frontier was becoming calm. Settlers continued to pour into the region.

Not surprisingly, Daniel was beginning to feel crowded in Boonesborough, and before long he moved to a new settlement on Limestone Creek, where he and Rebecca established a frontier inn, tavern, and general store of sorts. However, Daniel was as poor a tavern-keeper as he was a land speculator, and he never really made a go of the business. As usual, the endeavors that brought him the most joy were hunting and trapping.

Daniel's exploits eventually brought him fame. In 1784, fellow Kentuckian John Filson published "Discovery, Settlement and Present State of Kentucke and an Essay Towards the Topography, and Natural History of That Important Country."

Chief Joseph Brant was a Mowhawk leader who sided with the British against the American colonists. Late in 1781, Chief Brant led a large force into Kentucky. The Native Americans killed many of the settlers, including Daniel Boone's brother Squire.

Filson also included a 34-page autobiography about Boone, based on interviews he supposedly recorded. The account was widely circulated throughout the United States and Europe, and Daniel Boone became a frontier hero.

Kentucky became the 15th state of the Union on June 1, 1792. But in typical fashion, Daniel turned his sights further westward to new frontiers. The Spanish, who controlled the land west of the Mississippi River, encouraged Boone to settle in the Missouri territory. They promised him a huge ***tract*** of land, hoping that his presence would bring other settlers.

Now almost 65, Daniel set out on his latest adventure, with Rebecca and the children riding down the Ohio in a 60-foot canoe he had made from a poplar tree. Boone supposedly told a reporter in Cincinnati that he was leaving because Kentucky had grown too crowded.

He arrived in St. Louis in 1799 to much fanfare, and was appointed to hand out **land grants** to new settlers. In those days, pioneers received from 340 to 510 acres, with an additional 34 acres for each family member or slave. Daniel eventually ended up with 850 acres next to the property of his son, Daniel Morgan, about 60 miles west of St. Louis.

This region was known as the Femme Osage district. In 1800, Daniel was named *magistrate*–a minor judge–and given authority to settle local disputes. Daniel enjoyed some of his most prosperous years here, because he finally owned his own land in an area filled with wild game.

John Filson's 1784 history of Kentucky was just the first of many tales about Daniel Boone. Over the years books, movies, and television programs have been devoted to his life and adventures on the frontier.

The Spanish rewarded him for attracting additional settlers by increasing his land holdings ten different times. In many ways, Boone was at the peak of his power and prestige. But heartache came in March 1813, when his beloved wife Rebecca died at age 73, after years of enduring many hardships taming the frontier with her restless husband.

And Daniel's fortunes were also reversing on another front: after the United States bought the Louisiana Territory from France (which had purchased it from Spain), the government decided to abolish Boone's official position. The United States also refused to recognize his claim to the thousands of acres he had received from Spain. The U.S. government finally agreed to leave Daniel with his original 850-acre tract, but he was forced to sell the property to settle some debts.

He spent his final years of slowly deteriorating health canoeing the Missouri in search of furs and game to raise more money to pay his debt. The years began taking their toll. By age 84, he was staying closer to home, hindered by bouts of arthritis.

Finally, not long before his 86th birthday, Daniel Boone passed away. Supposedly, he died from a case of indigestion after eating too many sweet pota-

The legacy of Daniel Boone: after his death, settlers continued to push the frontier of the United States westward. Immigrants to America traveled to new territories in covered wagons like the ones pictured here.

toes, one of his favorite foods. America's most famous frontier explorer was taken back to Kentucky with the body of Rebecca and buried there.

Considering Boone's distaste for civilization, he probably would have preferred to be buried on the frontier of Missouri, although by then even this area was being settled by other pioneers who continued the relentless push westward.

Chronology

1712 Daniel Boone's father, Squire Boone, comes from England to Pennsylvania with his brother and sister.

1717 The entire Boone family migrates to Pennsylvania.

1734 Daniel Boone is born on November 2.

1754 French and Indian War begins.

1755 British general Edward Braddock is killed in poorly planned attack on Fort Duquesne.

1758 John Forbes, a British general, successfully leads a large army against Fort Duquesne.

1756 Daniel Boone and Rebecca Bryan are married in August.

1763 England attempts to restrict further colonial settlement west of the Appalachian Mountains.

1765 Boone travels to Florida with friends from militia and considers acquiring land there; Rebecca says no.

1767 Boone discovers the Cumberland Gap; visits Kentucky.

1775 Revolutionary War begins.

1776 The Declaration of Independence is written; Jemima Boone and two friends are captured by Indians, but are rescued.

1777 Daniel Boone is captured by Shawnee Indians; escapes to warn settlers in Boonesborough of impending attack.

1778 Indians attack Boonesborough unsuccessfully.

1779 Twenty thousand settlers migrate to Kentucky.

1784 John Filson publishes his book, which includes a short autobiography of Daniel Boone, making him a national and international celebrity.

1792   Kentucky is named the 15th state.

1799   Daniel and Rebecca Boone move to the Missouri Territory.

1803   The United States buys the Louisiana Territory from France for $15 million.

1813   Rebecca Boone dies in March.

1820   Daniel Boone passes away at age 85.

Glossary

allies–friendly nations that agree to help each other during wartime.

atrocities–extremely wicked or brutal acts.

campaign–an organized military operation.

captivity–imprisonment.

controversial–when the facts about someone or something are disputed and lead to argument.

court-martial–a trial for a person in the military.

frontier–the farthest borders of a country's settled area.

frontiersman–a person who lives on the frontier.

game–wild animals hunted by woodsmen, often for food.

land grants–areas of land given to settlers.

magistrate–a local judge, or justice of the peace.

massacre–a ruthless slaughter or killing.

militia–a citizen army.

outfit–to supply with equipment, clothes, and tools.

pelts–the untreated skin of a furbearing animal.

persecute–to oppress a person unfairly because of his or her opinions or beliefs.

preservative–a substance that keeps things from being destroyed (for example, salt is a preservative because it keeps meat from spoiling).

Quaker–a religious sect founded in the 17th century. Quakers refused to fight in wars, and felt they did not need priests or ministers to communicate with God.

rebellion–an organized resistance to authority.

skirmish–a minor battle between small groups of soldiers.

stockade–a small fort made with wooden posts or stakes.

strategy–skillful management in getting the better of an enemy.

tract–a region of indefinite extent.

trek–a difficult journey.

wanderlust–an overwhelming desire to journey.

weaver–a person who makes a living by weaving cloth.

Further Reading

Bakeless, John. *Daniel Boone.* New York: Morrow, 1919.

Daugherty, James. *Daniel Boone.* New York: The Viking Press, 1939.

Giles, Janice H. *The Kentuckians.* Lexington: University Press of Kentucky, 1988.

Lawlor, Laurie. *Daniel Boone.* Niles, IL: Whitman, Albert & Co., 1988.

Lofaro, Michael A. *The Life and Adventures of Daniel Boone.* Lexington: University Press of Kentucky, 1986.

Zadra, Dan. *Frontiersmen in America: Daniel Boone.* Mankato, MN: Creative Education, 1988.

Index

Picture Credits

RICHARD KOZAR has written several Chelsea House books, including biographies of Hillary Rodham Clinton and Elizabeth Dole. He is also the author of *Lewis and Clark: Explorers of the Louisiana Purchase* in the EXPLORERS OF NEW WORLDS series. He lives in Whitney, Pennsylvania, with his wife, Heidi, and daughters Caty and Macy.